Spotter's Guide to
WOODLAND LIFE

Edited by Sue Jacquemier

Illustrated by John Barber, Joyce Bee,
Trevor Boyer, Hilary Burn, William Giles,
Victoria Goaman, Andy Martin, Annabel Milne
& Peter Stebbing, Chris Shields, Phil Weare

Special Consultants
Ted Ellis, Esmond Harris, Anthony Wootton

USBORNE

Contents

The illustrations of trees, birds, mammals, wild flowers and insects in this book are taken from the original *Spotter's Guides to Trees, Birds, Animals Tracks & Signs, Wild Flowers and Insects*, also published by Usborne.

Designed by
Sally Burrough and
Cloud Nine Design

Consultants and contributors:
Jessica Datta, Esmond Harris,
Peter Holden, Chris Humphries,
Alfred Leutscher, Ruth Thomson

First published in 1979 by
Usborne Publishing Limited,
20 Garrick Street, London WC2

Text and Artwork ©1979 by
Usborne Publishing Limited

Made and printed in Great Britain
by Purnell & Sons Ltd,
Paulton (Bristol) and London

How to use this book

This book is an identification guide to the animals and plants found in British and European woodlands. Take it with you when you go out spotting, and each time you see a new animal or plant, tick it off in the small circle next to the appropriate illustration.

The book is divided into various sections: trees, wild flowers, ferns, fungi, mammals, birds, butterflies, moths and other insects. The descriptions next to the illustrations will help you identify the species (the kind, or type, of animal or plant) that you see.

What the illustrations show

 The illustrations of **trees** show the whole tree in summer and, if it is deciduous (a tree that loses its leaves every autumn), the whole tree in winter. They also show close-ups of the bark, and some leaves. Sometimes the flowers are shown, and the fruit. Cones are the fruits of coniferous trees, such as pine and fir.

 The illustrations of **wild flowers** sometimes have extra close-up pictures of the flower, its fruit or its seed.

 The male of some of the **birds** and **insects** (♂) is very different from the female (♀) and so both sexes have been illustrated.

 With the illustrations of the **mammals,** there are also pictures of the tracks they make.

There are many hundreds of different species of **fungi** (mushrooms and toadstools), and we have been able to illustrate only a few of the common ones in this book.

Some edible fungi look very similar to other species which are poisonous. Unless you have some detailed knowledge of fungi and are experienced in selecting edible species, **do not eat or taste** any that you find. Check first in a larger field guide (see p. 59) or ask someone who knows about fungi in order to learn more.

Scorecard

At the end of the book is a scorecard which awards you a score for each species of plant or animal that you spot. A very common species scores 5 points, whereas a very rare one is worth

SPECIES	SCORE	DATE SEEN
Red Fox	10	26th July

25 points. Count up your score after a day out spotting and see how many you can get.

Measuring plants and animals

The drawings on this page show you how animals and plants are measured. The measurements are normally average sizes, given in centimetres (cm) or metres (m) in the captions next to the illustrations. The plants and animals in this book are not drawn to scale, so their sizes will help you to identify the different species.

Birds. Length of bird from beak to tip of tail, given in centimetres.

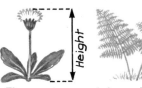

Flowers, trees and ferns. Height from ground level, in centimetres or metres.

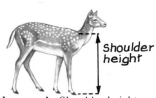

Hoofed mammals. Shoulder height (SH), given in metres or centimetres.

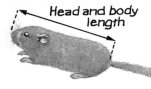

Small mammals. Length of head and body (H&B), not including tail, given in centimetres.

Butterflies and moths. Wing span (WS), given in centimetres.

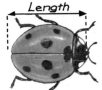

Other insects. Body length, not including antennae, given in centimetres.

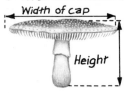

Fungi. Width of cap, or height from ground level, given in centimetres.

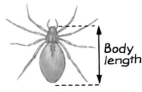

Spiders. Body length, not including legs, given in centimetres.

Conservation and wildlife

Conservation

Woodlands contain a wealth of animal- and plant-life which needs to be carefully protected if the balance of nature within woodlands is not to be upset. You can help by not damaging trees and other plants, and by not disturbing birds and other animals unnecessarily. Many of the wild flowers, birds and some mammals are protected by law.

It is illegal to dig up any wild plant unless you have permission to do so from the person who owns the land it is growing on. It is also illegal to pick certain rare flowers. Many wild plants that were once common are now rare, partly because people have picked so many of them.

If you pick wild flowers, they will die, but if you leave them where they are, you will be able to go and look at them again and again, and so will other people.

It is also illegal to disturb breeding birds, their nests or eggs, so be careful to watch from a distance, unnoticed by the birds.

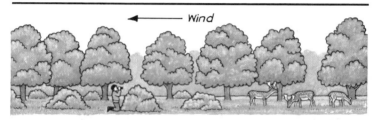

Wind ←

Watching wildlife

You will be able to see many more birds and animals in a wood if you walk very quietly, and keep out of sight as much as possible. Move slowly and try not to snap twigs underfoot. Step on mud or damp grass when you can, as this is quieter.

Wear dull-coloured clothes that merge with the background, and a hat that shades your face, making it less noticeable.

Use bushes and trees to hide behind, and once you spot an animal, stand completely still. Animals will often notice sudden movement before they see your shape.

If there is a breeze, position yourself so that the wind does not carry your scent to the animal, as this will warn it of your presence.

Binoculars are useful, but not essential, for bird- and animal-watching. Choose a pair with a magnification of x6 or x8, as these are easy to focus.

Take a notebook and pencils with you to jot down details of what the animals you see were doing. You could also make a note of the time of day, the date, and other information.

Trees

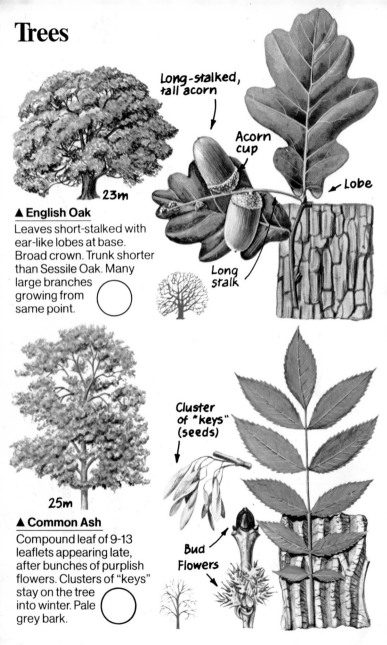

Long-stalked, tall acorn

Acorn cup

Lobe

▲ English Oak

Leaves short-stalked with ear-like lobes at base. Broad crown. Trunk shorter than Sessile Oak. Many large branches growing from same point.

Long stalk

23m

Cluster of "keys" (seeds)

Bud

Flowers

▲ Common Ash

Compound leaf of 9-13 leaflets appearing late, after bunches of purplish flowers. Clusters of "keys" stay on the tree into winter. Pale grey bark.

25m

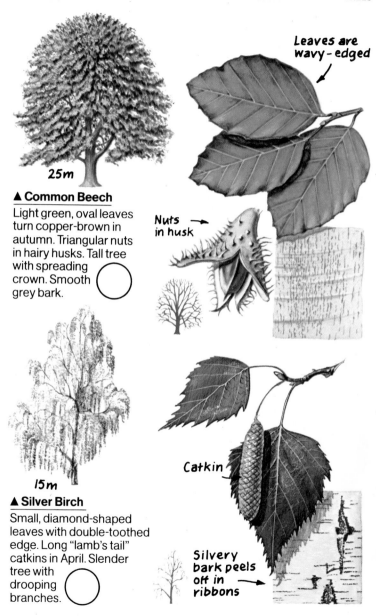

Leaves are
wavy-edged

25m

▲ Common Beech

Light green, oval leaves
turn copper-brown in
autumn. Triangular nuts
in hairy husks. Tall tree
with spreading
crown. Smooth
grey bark.

Nuts
in husk

15m

▲ Silver Birch

Small, diamond-shaped
leaves with double-toothed
edge. Long "lamb's tail"
catkins in April. Slender
tree with
drooping
branches.

Catkin

Silvery
bark peels
off in
ribbons

7

12m

▲ Common Alder
Leaves rounded, falling in
late autumn. Young twigs
and leaves sticky. Reddish
catkins. Fruits like small,
brown, woody
cones. Always
near water.

Leaf has
notched tip

Cone-like
fruit stays on
all winter

Toothed
edge

20m

▲ Sycamore
Dark green, leathery leaves
with five lobes. Paired,
closely-angled, winged
seeds. Large spreading
tree. Smooth
brown bark
becoming scaly.

Seeds twist
as they fall

Flowers

Clusters of 2-3 fruits containing nuts

25m

▲ Sweet Chestnut
Long narrow leaves with saw-toothed edge. Edible brown chestnuts in green prickly case. Spiral-furrowed bark. Large, tall-crowned tree.

Berries

One flower (from a cluster)

Toothed edge

7m

▲ Rowan
Compound leaf like Ash, but smaller. Clusters of creamy-white flowers in May. Red berries ripen in August. Small tree. Often grows alone on mountainsides.

Leaves turn red in autumn

9

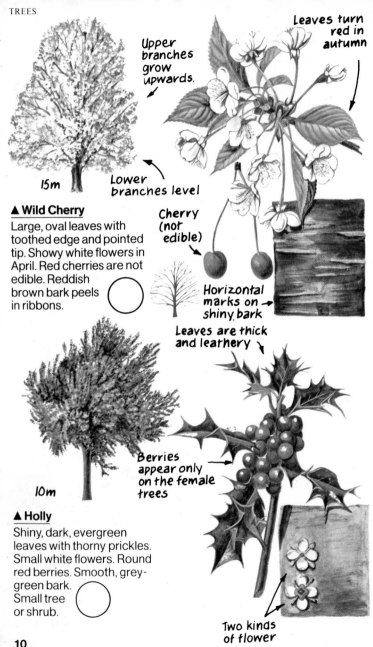

Upper
branches
grow
upwards.

Leaves turn
red in
autumn

Lower
branches level

15m

▲ Wild Cherry

Large, oval leaves with
toothed edge and pointed
tip. Showy white flowers in
April. Red cherries are not
edible. Reddish
brown bark peels
in ribbons.

Cherry
(not
edible)

Horizontal
marks on
shiny bark

Leaves are thick
and leathery

Berries
appear only
on the female
trees

10m

▲ Holly

Shiny, dark, evergreen
leaves with thorny prickles.
Small white flowers. Round
red berries. Smooth, grey-
green bark.
Small tree
or shrub.

Two kinds
of flower

10

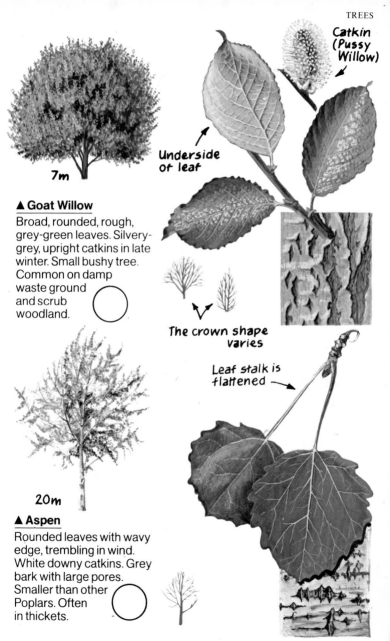

Catkin
(Pussy
Willow)

Underside
of leaf

▲ Goat Willow

Broad, rounded, rough, grey-green leaves. Silvery-grey, upright catkins in late winter. Small bushy tree. Common on damp waste ground and scrub woodland.

The crown shape varies

Leaf stalk is flattened →

7m

20m

▲ Aspen

Rounded leaves with wavy edge, trembling in wind. White downy catkins. Grey bark with large pores. Smaller than other Poplars. Often in thickets.

11

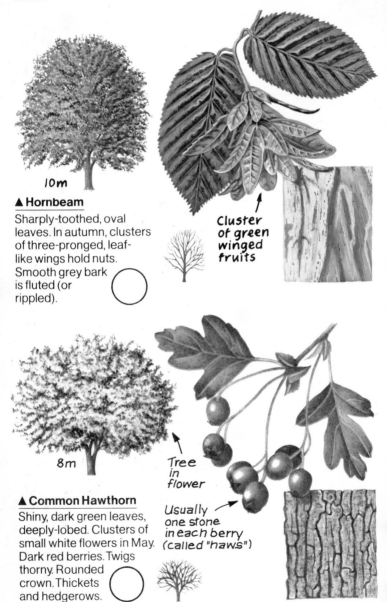

10m

▲ Hornbeam

Sharply-toothed, oval leaves. In autumn, clusters of three-pronged, leaf-like wings hold nuts. Smooth grey bark is fluted (or rippled).

Cluster of green winged fruits

8m

Tree in flower

▲ Common Hawthorn

Shiny, dark green leaves, deeply-lobed. Clusters of small white flowers in May. Dark red berries. Twigs thorny. Rounded crown. Thickets and hedgerows.

Usually one stone in each berry (called "haws")

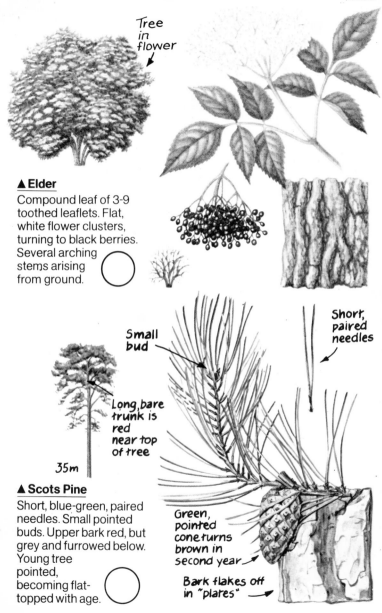

Tree in flower

▲ Elder
Compound leaf of 3-9 toothed leaflets. Flat, white flower clusters, turning to black berries. Several arching stems arising from ground.

Small bud

Long, bare trunk is red near top of tree

35m

Short, paired needles

▲ Scots Pine
Short, blue-green, paired needles. Small pointed buds. Upper bark red, but grey and furrowed below. Young tree pointed, becoming flat-topped with age.

Green, pointed cone turns brown in second year

Bark flakes off in "plates"

13

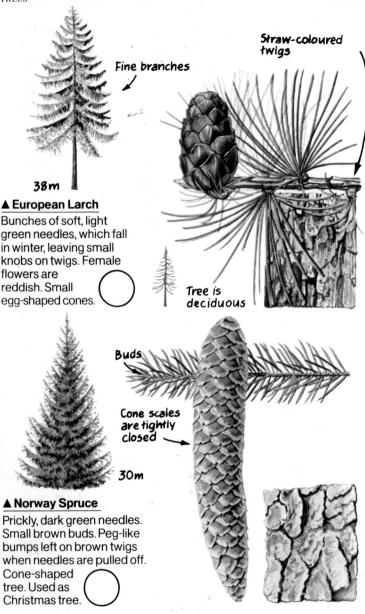

Fine branches

Straw-coloured twigs

38m

▲ European Larch

Bunches of soft, light green needles, which fall in winter, leaving small knobs on twigs. Female flowers are reddish. Small egg-shaped cones.

Tree is deciduous

Buds

Cone scales are tightly closed ←

30m

▲ Norway Spruce

Prickly, dark green needles. Small brown buds. Peg-like bumps left on brown twigs when needles are pulled off. Cone-shaped tree. Used as Christmas tree.

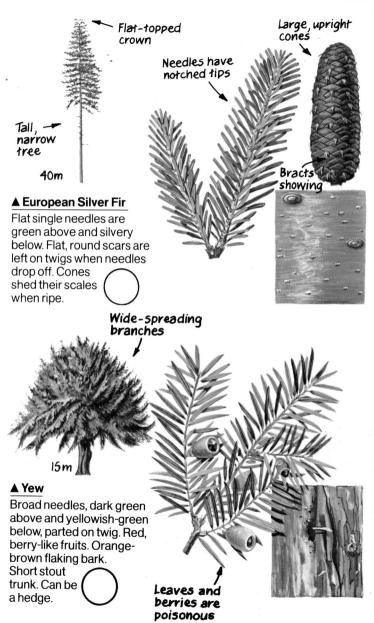

Flat-topped crown

Large, upright cones

Needles have notched tips

Tall, narrow tree
40m

Bracts showing

▲ European Silver Fir

Flat single needles are green above and silvery below. Flat, round scars are left on twigs when needles drop off. Cones shed their scales when ripe.

Wide-spreading branches

▲ Yew

Broad needles, dark green above and yellowish-green below, parted on twig. Red, berry-like fruits. Orange-brown flaking bark. Short stout trunk. Can be a hedge.

15m

Leaves and berries are poisonous

Birds

◀ Nightjar

Rarely seen in daylight. Listen for its continuous churring after dark when it hunts insects. Summer migrant. Woods and heaths. 27 cm.

Sparrowhawk ▶

Broad-winged hawk. Hunts small birds along hedges and woodland edges. Never hovers. Female 38 cm. Male 30 cm.

♂

Notice the pale wing patches

◀ Buzzard

A large bird of prey with broad rounded wings. Often seen soaring over moors and farmland as it hunts. Rare in south and eastern England. 54 cm.

Tawny Owl ▶

Calls with familiar "hoot". Hunts at night where there are woods or old trees. Eats small mammals or birds. 38 cm.

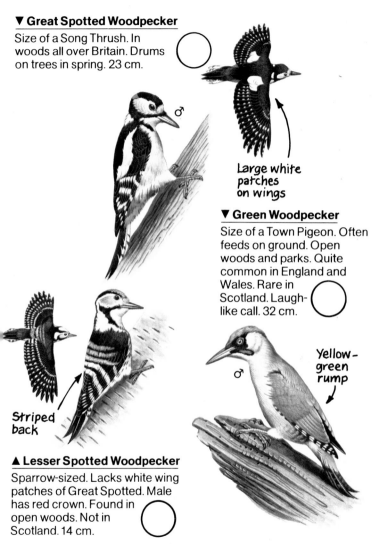

▼ Great Spotted Woodpecker
Size of a Song Thrush. In woods all over Britain. Drums on trees in spring. 23 cm.

♂

Large white patches on wings

▼ Green Woodpecker
Size of a Town Pigeon. Often feeds on ground. Open woods and parks. Quite common in England and Wales. Rare in Scotland. Laugh-like call. 32 cm.

♂

Yellow-green rump

Striped back

▲ Lesser Spotted Woodpecker
Sparrow-sized. Lacks white wing patches of Great Spotted. Male has red crown. Found in open woods. Not in Scotland. 14 cm.

Woodpeckers do not live in Ireland. They all have bouncing flight

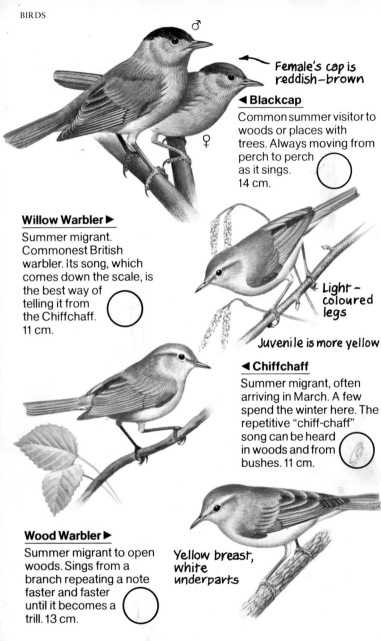

Female's cap is reddish-brown

◀ Blackcap

Common summer visitor to woods or places with trees. Always moving from perch to perch as it sings. 14 cm.

Willow Warbler ▶

Summer migrant. Commonest British warbler. Its song, which comes down the scale, is the best way of telling it from the Chiffchaff. 11 cm.

Light-coloured legs

Juvenile is more yellow

◀ Chiffchaff

Summer migrant, often arriving in March. A few spend the winter here. The repetitive "chiff-chaff" song can be heard in woods and from bushes. 11 cm.

Wood Warbler ▶

Summer migrant to open woods. Sings from a branch repeating a note faster and faster until it becomes a trill. 13 cm.

Yellow breast, white underparts

Northern and Eastern Europe

Britain and Western Europe

◀ Long-tailed Tit

Hedgerows and woodland edges are good places to see groups of these tiny birds. 14 cm.

Marsh Tit ▶

A bird of deciduous woods, like the Willow Tit (not illustrated). Rarely visits gardens. 11 cm.

No pale patch on wings

Brown above, paler below

◀ Garden Warbler

Summer visitor. Sings from dense cover, and is hard to see. Likes woods with undergrowth or thick hedges. Song can be confused with Blackcap's. 14 cm.

Coal Tit ▶

Likes conifer woods, but often seen in deciduous trees. Large white patch on back of head. 11 cm.

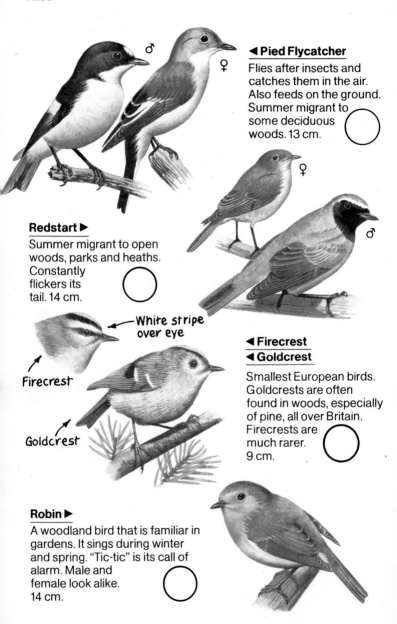

◄ Pied Flycatcher

Flies after insects and catches them in the air. Also feeds on the ground. Summer migrant to some deciduous woods. 13 cm.

♂ ♀

Redstart ►

Summer migrant to open woods, parks and heaths. Constantly flickers its tail. 14 cm.

♀ ♂

White stripe over eye

Firecrest

Goldcrest

◄ Firecrest
◄ Goldcrest

Smallest European birds. Goldcrests are often found in woods, especially of pine, all over Britain. Firecrests are much rarer. 9 cm.

Robin ►

A woodland bird that is familiar in gardens. It sings during winter and spring. "Tic-tic" is its call of alarm. Male and female look alike. 14 cm.

Chaffinch ▶

Likely to be found wherever there are trees and bushes, including gardens. Often flocks with other finches in winter.
15 cm.

♀

♂

◀ Crossbill

Nests in Scottish pine woods. Rare elsewhere. Eats seeds from pine cones. 16 cm.

♀   ♂

Sparrow-sized

Siskin ▶

A small finch. Nests in conifers. Visits gardens in winter to feed on peanuts.
11 cm.

♀   ♂

Mealy Redpoll

Lesser Redpoll

◀ Lesser Redpoll
◀ Mealy Redpoll

The Lesser Redpoll is common in birch woods and forestry plantations in Britain. The Mealy lives in northern Europe. 12 cm.

21

◀ Treecreeper
Usually seen in woods climbing up tree trunks and flying down again to search for food. Listen for its high-pitched call. 13 cm.

Jay ▶
Secretive woodland bird. Will visit gardens. Listen for its harsh screeching call. Look for white rump in flight. 32 cm.

◀ Nuthatch
Found in deciduous woods in England and Wales. Climbs up and down trees in a series of short hops. Very short tail. Nests in tree-holes. 14 cm.

Woodpigeon ▶
A common bird of farmland, woods and towns. Forms large flocks in winter. 41 cm.

White on wings

Pheasant ▶

Lives on farmland with hedges. Often reared and shot as game. Roosts in trees. Nests on ground. Look for the long tail. Male 87 cm. Female 58 cm.

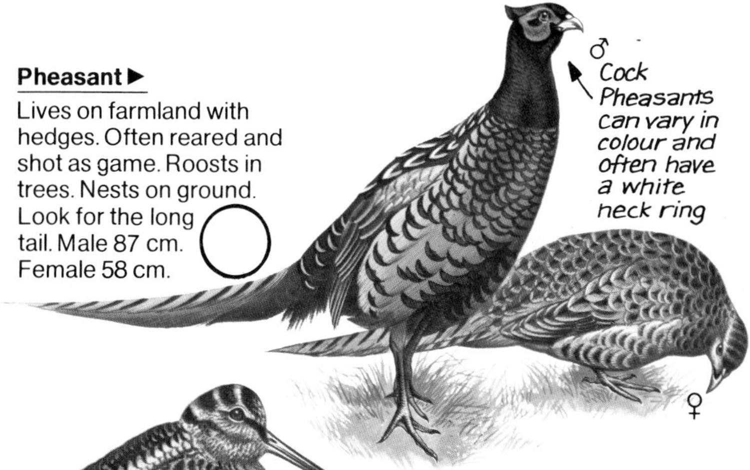

♂ *Cock Pheasants can vary in colour and often have a white neck ring*

♀

◀ Woodcock

Secretive bird of damp woods. Watch out for its display flight over woods at dusk in early summer. 34 cm.

Capercaillie ▶

This large bird lives in coniferous forests in parts of Scotland. Eats pine shoots at tips of branches. Male 86 cm. Female 61 cm.

♂

♀

Mammals

Red Deer ▶
Lives in herds in open country and woods. Young ("calves") are spotted. Eats grass, heather, fruit, tree bark and may raid crops. SH 1.5 m.

Summer coat

♂

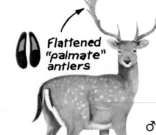

Flattened "palmate" antlers

♂

◀ Fallow Deer
Lives in herds in parks and woods. Fawns are heavily spotted. Eats grass, acorns, buds, bark, berries and fungi. SH 1 m.

Summer coat

♂

Roe Deer ▶
Grey-brown in winter. Lives on its own or in small groups in conifer plantations, near water. Eats leaves, berries, herbs. SH 70 cm.

Fore foot   Hind foot

◀ Red Fox
Common in woodlands and farmland. Usually nocturnal. Catches small mammals, birds, young deer, etc. H&B 65 cm.

Badger ▶

Nocturnal. Mainly in woods. Lives in family group in underground sett. Eats mainly worms, roots, small animals, plants, etc. H&B 80 cm.

Fore foot   *Hind foot*

◀ Polecat

Wooded country, often near houses. Rare in Britain. Eats small mammals, eggs, frogs, etc. Nocturnal and solitary. H&B 40 cm.

Hind foot   *Fore foot*

Wild Cat ▶

Remote woody areas in Scotland and parts of Europe. Nocturnal and shy. Ambushes mountain animals like hares, grouse. H&B 65 cm.

Fore foot   Hind foot

Broad head

Fore foot   Hind foot

◀ Pine Marten

Mountain woods (chiefly coniferous). Shy and nocturnal. Good climber. Eats birds, insects, small mammals, berries. H&B 50 cm.

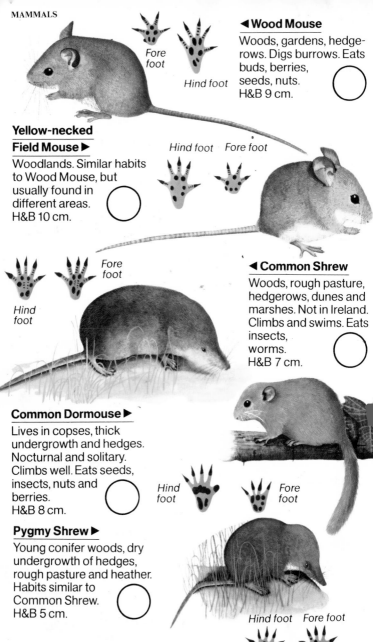

◀ Wood Mouse

Woods, gardens, hedgerows. Digs burrows. Eats buds, berries, seeds, nuts.
H&B 9 cm.

Fore foot

Hind foot

Yellow-necked
Field Mouse ▶

Woodlands. Similar habits to Wood Mouse, but usually found in different areas.
H&B 10 cm.

Hind foot   *Fore foot*

Fore foot

Hind foot

◀ Common Shrew

Woods, rough pasture, hedgerows, dunes and marshes. Not in Ireland. Climbs and swims. Eats insects, worms.
H&B 7 cm.

Common Dormouse ▶

Lives in copses, thick undergrowth and hedges. Nocturnal and solitary. Climbs well. Eats seeds, insects, nuts and berries.
H&B 8 cm.

Hind foot   *Fore foot*

Pygmy Shrew ▶

Young conifer woods, dry undergrowth of hedges, rough pasture and heather. Habits similar to Common Shrew.
H&B 5 cm.

Hind foot   Fore foot

Fore foot

Hind foot

Ear tufts

Fore foot

Hind foot

▲ Grey Squirrel

Coat may have patches of brown in summer. Much bolder than Red Squirrel.
H&B 27 cm.

▲ Red Squirrel

Mostly in coniferous woods. Eats seeds of cones, buds, berries, bark, nuts, etc.
H&B 23 cm.

◄ Rabbit

Woodland, hillsides and dunes. Eats plants.
H&B 40 cm.

Fore foot

Hind foot

Fore foot   Hind foot

Brown Hare ►

Woodland, open farmland. Usually solitary and silent. Rests above ground in a hollow called a "form."
H&B 58 cm.

Long ears with black tips

It has longer legs than a rabbit

Edible fungi

Fungi grow in woodlands of all kinds, mainly on decaying leaf litter and rotting wood. If you are not sure that a mushroom or toadstool is edible, do not eat or taste it.

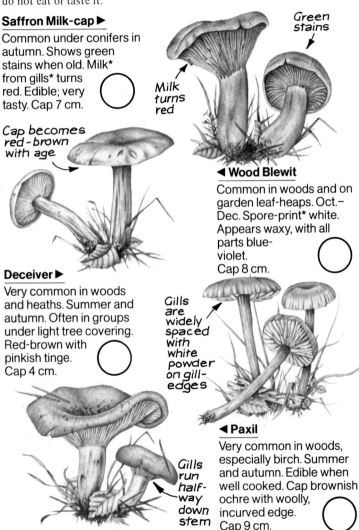

Saffron Milk-cap ▶

Common under conifers in autumn. Shows green stains when old. Milk* from gills* turns red. Edible; very tasty. Cap 7 cm.

Green stains

Milk turns red

Cap becomes red-brown with age

Deceiver ▶

Very common in woods and heaths. Summer and autumn. Often in groups under light tree covering. Red-brown with pinkish tinge. Cap 4 cm.

◀ Wood Blewit

Common in woods and on garden leaf-heaps. Oct.– Dec. Spore-print* white. Appears waxy, with all parts blue-violet. Cap 8 cm.

Gills are widely spaced with white powder on gill-edges

◀ Paxil

Very common in woods, especially birch. Summer and autumn. Edible when well cooked. Cap brownish ochre with woolly, incurved edge. Cap 9 cm.

Gills run halfway down stem

28

*see Glossary, page 58

Edible fungi

Gills run down stem

◄ Chanterelle
Often in groups on mossy ground, woods and heaths. Summer and autumn. Bright yellow all over; has mild apricot fragrance. Firm in texture. Cap 7 cm.

Wood Mushroom ►
Fairly common; grows mainly under conifers. Summer and autumn. Cap has smooth, reddish-brown scales. Has strong almond scent. Cap 7 cm.

Broad ring on stem ↘

◄ Cep
Common under broad-leaved trees, especially beech. Autumn. Cap sticky when moist. Stem has white net of veins. Cap 13 cm.

Honey Fungus ►
A common killer of trees. Develops luminous sheets and bootlace-like strands that spread under bark. To be eaten in moderation. Cap 8 cm.

Grows in clumps from stumps and trunks ↘

Poisonous and inedible fungi

A few fungi are dangerously poisonous; it is important that you should be able to recognize them. Some other fungi have a nasty smell or taste, making them unfit to eat.

Funnel-cap ▶

Fairly common in woods and on heaths. Summer and autumn. Slightly silky cap and hairs at stem-base.
Cap 6 cm.

Funnel-shaped cap

Bright red cap

Red Milk-cap ▶

Very common under pines. Summer and autumn. Gills* contain white, bitter milk* making it too peppery to eat. Cap 6 cm.

◀ Sickener

Common under birch and pine. Late summer and autumn. Brittle white gills* Has a sickening, peppery taste when raw.
Cap 7 cm.

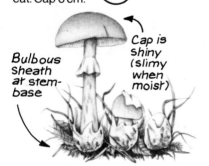

Bulbous sheath at stem-base

Cap is shiny (slimy when moist)

◀ Death-cap

Grows mainly under beech and oak. Aug.–Sept. **Deadly.** Cap is streaked brownish olive or primrose yellow. Gills, stalk and ring are white.
Cap 9 cm.

*see Glossary, page 58

Poisonous and inedible fungi

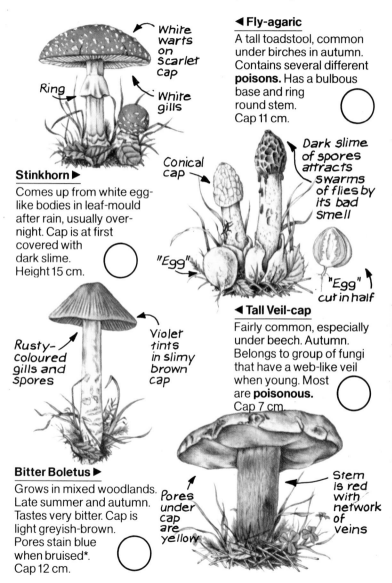

White warts on scarlet cap

Ring

White gills

◀ Fly-agaric
A tall toadstool, common under birches in autumn. Contains several different **poisons.** Has a bulbous base and ring round stem. Cap 11 cm.

Stinkhorn ▶
Comes up from white egg-like bodies in leaf-mould after rain, usually over-night. Cap is at first covered with dark slime. Height 15 cm.

Conical cap

Dark slime of spores attracts swarms of flies by its bad smell

"Egg"

"Egg" cut in half

◀ Tall Veil-cap
Fairly common, especially under beech. Autumn. Belongs to group of fungi that have a web-like veil when young. Most are **poisonous.** Cap 7 cm.

Rusty-coloured gills and spores

Violet tints in slimy brown cap

Stem is red with network of veins

Bitter Boletus ▶
Grows in mixed woodlands. Late summer and autumn. Tastes very bitter. Cap is light greyish-brown. Pores stain blue when bruised*. Cap 12 cm.

Pores under cap are yellow

Wild flowers

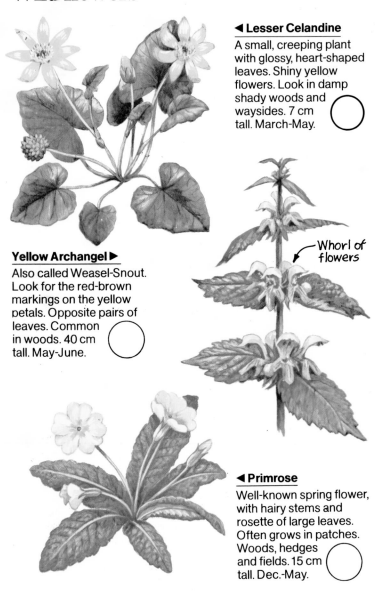

A small, creeping plant with glossy, heart-shaped leaves. Shiny yellow flowers. Look in damp shady woods and waysides. 7 cm tall. March-May.

Yellow Archangel ▶
Also called Weasel-Snout. Look for the red-brown markings on the yellow petals. Opposite pairs of leaves. Common in woods. 40 cm tall. May-June.

Whorl of flowers

◀ **Primrose**
Well-known spring flower, with hairy stems and rosette of large leaves. Often grows in patches. Woods, hedges and fields. 15 cm tall. Dec.-May.

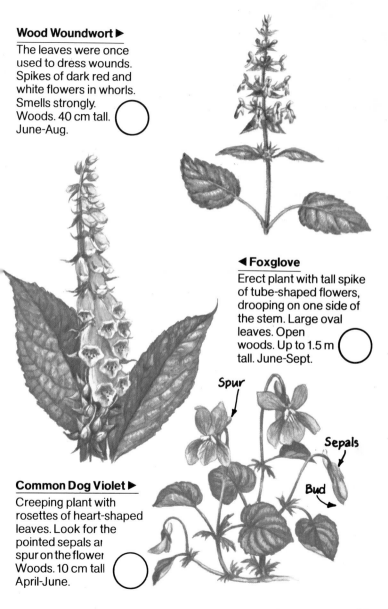

Wood Woundwort ▶

The leaves were once used to dress wounds. Spikes of dark red and white flowers in whorls. Smells strongly. Woods. 40 cm tall. June-Aug.

◀ Foxglove

Erect plant with tall spike of tube-shaped flowers, drooping on one side of the stem. Large oval leaves. Open woods. Up to 1.5 m tall. June-Sept.

Spur

Sepals

Bud

Common Dog Violet ▶

Creeping plant with rosettes of heart-shaped leaves. Look for the pointed sepals and spur on the flower. Woods. 10 cm tall April-June.

33

Flower bud

Lesser Periwinkle ▶

Creeps along the ground
with long runners, making
leafy carpets. Shiny oval
leaves. Woods and hedges.
Flower stems up
to 15 cm tall.
Feb.-May.

Runner

Runner

◀ Bluebell

Also called Wild Hyacinth.
Narrow, shiny leaves and
clusters of nodding blue
flowers. Forms thick
carpets in woods.
30 cm tall.
April-May.

Close-up
of fruit

Close-up of
bugle-shaped
flower

Bugle ▶

Creeping plant with erect
flower spikes. Purplish
stem is hairy on two
sides. Forms carpets in
damp woods.
10-20 cm tall.
May-June.

◀ Wood Sorrel

A creeping woodland plant with slender stems and rounded leaves. The white flowers have purplish veins. Woods and hedges. 10 cm tall. April-May.

Wild Strawberry ▶

Small plant with long, arching runners and oval, toothed leaves in threes. Sweet red fruits, covered with seeds. Woods and scrubland. April-July.

The large sepals look like petals

◀ Wood Anemone

Also called Granny's Nightcap. Forms carpets in woods. The flowers have pink-streaked sepals. 15 cm tall. March-June.

Dog's Mercury ▶

Downy plant with opposite, toothed leaves. Strong smelling. Male flowers grow on separate plants from female flowers. Found in patches in woodlands. 15–20 cm tall. Feb.–April.

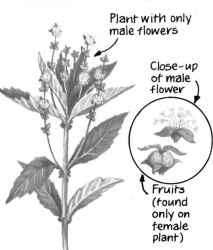

Plant with only male flowers

Close-up of male flower

Fruits (found only on female plant)

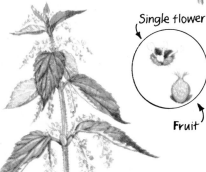

Single flower

Fruit

◀ Nettle

The toothed leaves are covered with stinging hairs. Dangling green-brown flowers. Used to make beer and tea. Common. Up to 1 m tall. June-Aug.

Cuckoo Pint/Lords and Ladies ▶

The flowers are hidden inside the green hood. The leaves sometimes have dark spots. Likes shady woods and hedgerows. Up to 45 cm tall. Flowers April-May.

Hood

Fruit is poisonous and can be seen in autumn

Ferns

Bracken ▶

Broad, light green feather fronds, becoming rust-coloured in autumn. Dies back in winter. On heaths and in open woods on well-drained, acid soils. Avoids wet ground.

Fronds are commonly 30cm long

Fronds are normally 1-2m tall

◀ Polypody

Fronds remain green in winter, with small rounded spore-patches underneath. Often in large clumps on banks; sometimes perched on mossy trees.

Hard Fern ▶

Stiff, shiny light green fronds. The longer ones in the middle are fertile (spore-bearing). Acid, peaty soils of woods, banks and hillsides. Favoured by moist climate.

Longer fronds are 30-90cm

◀ Hartstongue

Ribbon-like fronds light green, glossy when young, dark and leathery when old. Often plentiful in woodland shade where it is mild and moist.

Fronds up to 90cm long

Butterflies

Speckled Wood ▶

Likes bramble flowers.
Often settles on sun-
spotted leaves in woods
and forests.
Larva
eats grasses.
W.S. 47-50 mm.

♀

*Orange-brown
European form
of the Speckled
Wood*

♂

Comma ▲

Easy to recognize by its
ragged wing edges and the
shape of the letter "c" on
underside of its wings.
In woods and
gardens.
W.S. 56-58 mm.

White Admiral ▼

Flies around tree tops,
but may come down to
drink from mud or to visit
flowers like bramble.
Larva feeds on
honeysuckle.
W.S. 44-58 mm.

♂

♂

Purple Emperor ▶

One of Britain's largest
butterflies. Drinks from
woodland puddles. Males
fly around the tree tops.
Larva eats goat
willow leaves.
W.S. 76-84 mm.

Purple
sheen
on wings
is visible
when sun
shines
on them

♀

♂

♀

Thistle

◀ High Brown Fritillary

Very fond of thistle flowers.
In woods, where it may
sleep on high branches on
dull days. Larva eats
violet leaves.
W.S. 60-68 mm.

♀
♂
♀
♂

◀ Holly Blue

Visits holly and ivy flowers
and may drink by edges of
streams. Gardens and
woods. Larva feeds on
unripe berries of
holly and ivy.
W.S. 33-35 mm.

Holly

Moths

A variety of moths are found in woodlands during the summer months. Few are active during the day; they lie up on tree trunks or amid foliage, but many will come to artificial light after dark.

Leopard Moth ▶
Females can sometimes be seen resting on tree trunks. Larva is rarely seen as it feeds in the wood of various trees. Female W.S. 65 mm. Male W.S. 40 mm.

◀ Goat Moth
Widespread, but well camouflaged and rarely seen. Larva eats wood of ash and willow; spends three to four years in a tree trunk. It smells of goats. W.S. 70-85 mm.

Peach Blossom ▶
Found in woodland. Name comes from pattern on wings. Often attracted by "sugaring". Larva feeds on bramble. W.S. 35 mm.

Peach blossom pattern

◀ Merveille-du-Jour
Oak woodlands. Forewings match background of tree bark making moth difficult for enemies to see. Larva eats oak leaves. W.S. 45 mm.

Moths

◄ Peppered Moth

Usual spotted form may be replaced by a black form in some areas. Twig-like larva feeds on leaves of many trees. You may also find it on rose bushes.
W.S. 50-55 mm.

Bordered White ►

Males are dark brown with yellowish-white blotches. Larva feeds on conifers and can do a great deal of damage.
W.S. 30-35 mm.

♀

◄ Green Oak Tortrix

Larva common in midsummer, feeding on oak leaves. Each one feeds inside a rolled-up leaf; suspends itself from a silk thread if disturbed.
W.S. 20 mm.

Pine Hawk Moth ►

Fairly common in conifer woods; rests on tree trunks. Larva feeds on needles of conifers.
W.S. 70-90 mm.

41

Beetles

Some beetles, such as longhorns, visit flowers during the day. Others, such as the metallic-coloured leaf-beetles, occur in low vegetation. Many beetles can be found under bark, stones or in leaf-litter.

Nut Weevil ▶

Female uses her long rostrum (or snout) to pierce a young hazel-nut where she lays her single egg. Larva grows inside the nut eating the kernel.
10 mm long.

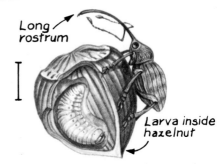

Long rostrum

Larva inside hazelnut

◀ Pine Weevil

On various conifers including pine and spruce. Adults eat young shoots. Eggs are laid in old tree stumps; larvae feed on bark and wood.
10-15 mm long.

Leaf-rolling Weevil ▶

Adults roll up birch and alder leaves and lay eggs inside. Larvae hatch and eat these leaves.
3-5 mm long.

Weevil cuts leaf in two places

1

2

3

It rolls leaf into a tube

Eggs are laid inside

Beetles

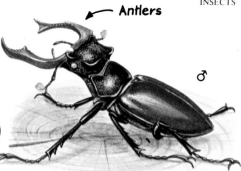

Antlers

♂

Stag Beetle ▶
Largest British beetle.
Only male has antlers.
Larva feeds in tree
stumps for three
years or more.
25-75 mm long.

◀ Ant Beetle
Small, fast-moving beetle
found on elms and conifers.
Larvae live under loose
bark and, like adults,
eat larvae
of bark beetles.
7-10 mm long.

Longhorn Beetle ▶
May be seen on flowers
along woodland paths. Flies
with wing cases raised and
makes a buzzing noise.
Larvae feed in
old tree stumps.
15-20 mm long.

◀ Elm Bark Beetle
Found on elm trees.
Female lays eggs along
the sides of a tunnel in
the wood; larvae burrow
at right angles
to it.
3-4 mm long.

Tunnels
made by
larvae

43

Beetles

◀ Violet Ground Beetle

Under large stones or undergrowth; common in woods and under hedges. Adult and larva eat other insects and worms. Larva pupates in soil.
30-35 mm long.

Eyed Ladybird ▶

Largest ladybird in Britain. Found near or on fir trees. Both adults and larvae hunt for aphids and scale-insects.
8-9 mm long.

Fir

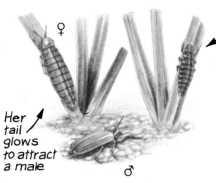

Larva

Her tail glows to attract a male

♀

♂

◀ Glow-worm

Open woods, grassy banks, hillsides. Most common in S. England. Wingless female attracts male with her glowing tail.
Male 15 mm long.
Female 20 mm long.

Bugs, Cricket

Common Shield Bug ▶

On oak and alder, also
fruit trees. Adults use
their "beaks" to pierce
and suck tissues of
caterpillars and
other larvae.
15 mm long.

◀ Spruce Aphid

Pineapple
gall

One generation of eggs
are laid on spruce shoots,
the next on larch, the next
on spruce, and so on.
Feeding of larvae causes
swellings, called
galls, on the shoots.
1-2 mm long.

Scale Insect ▶

Larvae live in little shells
on leaves, stems and fruits
of various trees. The wingless females (as well as
larvae) feed under these
scaly shells.
2-3 mm long.

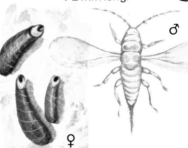

♂

♀

◀ Wood Cricket

In leaf litter, on paths, banks
and in ditches in S. England.
Male has a quiet, churring
song. Flightless.
8-9 mm long.

Sawflies, Wasps, etc.

Giant Wood Wasp/
Horntail ▶

Female lays eggs in sickly
or felled conifers. Larvae
feed on wood for up to
three years.
25-32 mm long.

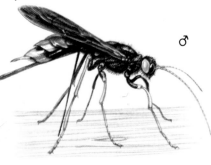

♂

♀

◀ Ichneumon Fly

A wasp, not a fly. Female
pierces pine trees with
her ovipositor (egg-layer)
and lays an egg on a
Horntail larva
inside the tree.
22-30 mm long.

Hornet ▶

Nests in hollow trees,
banks or roofs. Preys on
soft-bodied insects and
feeds them to its larvae.
Also feeds from
flowers in woods.
22-30 mm long.

Dog rose

*Sawfly larva
has nine pairs
of legs. Moth
larvae have
eight
pairs*

◀ Birch Sawfly

Name comes from
female's saw-like ovipositor.
Larva feeds on birch
leaves in late summer.
It makes an oval cocoon
from which the adult
emerges the
next spring.
20-22 mm long.

Ant, Centipede, Millipede

Wood Ant ▶

Makes a large, conical nest
from twigs and leaves in
pine woods. Cannot sting,
but sprays formic acid at
intruders. Thousands of
ants live in
each nest.
5-11 mm long.

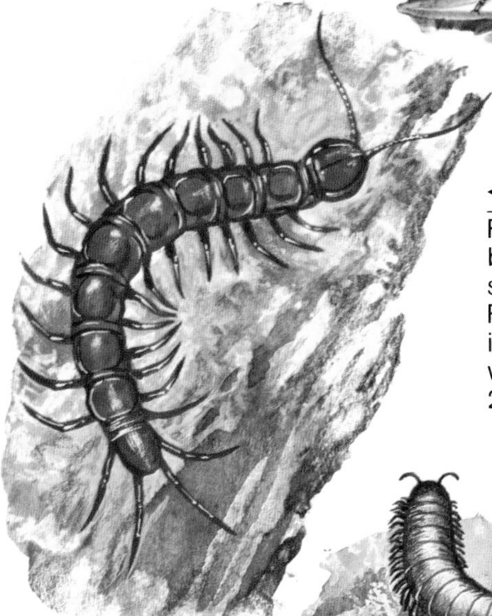

◀ Centipede

Found under leaf litter,
bark of old trees and
stumps, stones and in soil.
Feeds on all sorts of small
insects, larvae,
worms etc.
20-30 mm long.

Millipede ▶

Found under bark, leaf
litter where it is damp.
Usually about 100
pairs of legs.
30 mm long.

Spiders

Webs of spiders usually have a special shape and position which is distinct for each group. Not all woodland spiders make webs. Some hunt for prey on tree trunks or lie in wait on flowers.

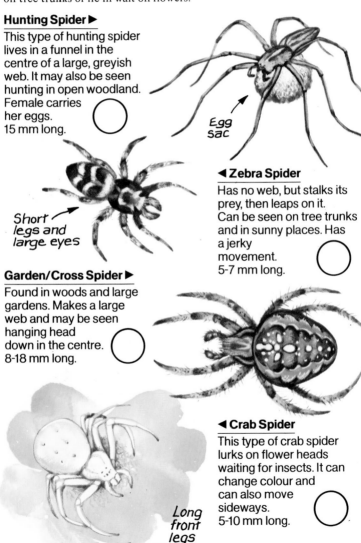

Hunting Spider ▶

This type of hunting spider lives in a funnel in the centre of a large, greyish web. It may also be seen hunting in open woodland. Female carries her eggs.
15 mm long.

Egg sac

Short legs and large eyes

Zebra Spider ◀

Has no web, but stalks its prey, then leaps on it. Can be seen on tree trunks and in sunny places. Has a jerky movement.
5-7 mm long.

Garden/Cross Spider ▶

Found in woods and large gardens. Makes a large web and may be seen hanging head down in the centre.
8-18 mm long.

Crab Spider ◀

This type of crab spider lurks on flower heads waiting for insects. It can change colour and can also move sideways.
5-10 mm long.

Long front legs

Reading tree stumps

The rings on a tree stump can tell you the age of the tree and give you an idea of the conditions which affected its growth.

Look at the rings with a magnifying glass. You can see how each one is made up of a light-coloured, soft layer, which is laid down in spring, and a dark, hard layer which is laid down in summer.

When there is lots of sun and water the tree will grow well and lay down lots of wood to form wide rings. If there is a drought, or the tree is too near other trees and cannot get enough sun, it will lay down narrow rings.

You may get a better idea of what caused particular patterns by comparing trees in the same area.

This tree's story is recorded in its annual rings

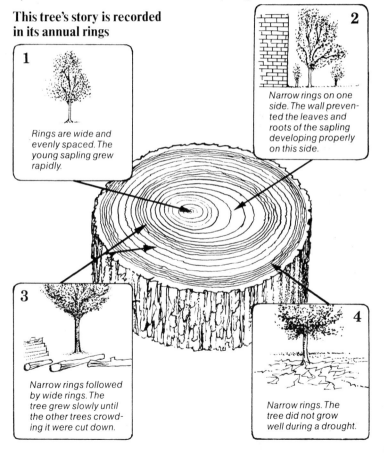

1 Rings are wide and evenly spaced. The young sapling grew rapidly.

2 Narrow rings on one side. The wall prevented the leaves and roots of the sapling developing properly on this side.

3 Narrow rings followed by wide rings. The tree grew slowly until the other trees crowding it were cut down.

4 Narrow rings. The tree did not grow well during a drought.

Woodlands

There are two main types of woodland – coniferous, made up chiefly of conifer trees, and broadleaved, made up chiefly of broadleaved trees. Conifer trees usually have needle- or scale-like leaves; their fruits are normally woody cones. Most are evergreens, but some, like larches, drop their leaves. Broadleaved trees bear fruit such as nuts, pods, and berries; the seed is inside these fruits. Most broadleaved trees in Britain are deciduous (that is, they drop their leaves in autumn), but some, like the holly, are evergreen.

Coniferous woods and forests

In coniferous forests it is dark all the year round because the trees do not drop all their leaves in autumn, as broadleaved trees do. This prevents the growth of many plants. Only mosses, ferns and fungi grow well here.

Conifers are good timber trees because they grow straight and tall; this makes them easy to saw into long planks. Plantations (woods planted for timber) of conifers or broadleaved trees are easy to recognize because the trees are usually planted in straight lines.

Cones

Only conifer trees bear cones. The seeds grow under the scales of the cone; when the cone is ripe, the scales open and the seeds are blown away.

Leaves

Conifer needles grow either in bundles, or singly; other conifer leaves are like tiny scales.

Scale ◄

NORWAY SPRUCE
Cone

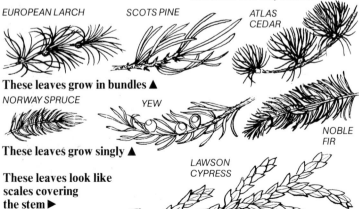

EUROPEAN LARCH   SCOTS PINE

ATLAS CEDAR

These leaves grow in bundles ▲

NORWAY SPRUCE   YEW

NOBLE FIR

These leaves grow singly ▲

These leaves look like scales covering the stem ▶

LAWSON CYPRESS

50

Life in a coniferous wood

Coniferous forests provide shelter for shy animals such as deer, and a home for birds such as treecreepers and goldcrests. This picture shows some of the animals and other wildlife you might spot in a coniferous wood.

LONG-EARED OWL

CROSSBILL

GOLDCREST

RED DEER

TREECREEPER

WOOD MUSHROOM

RED SQUIRREL

BROAD BUCKLER FERN

RED MILK-CAP

SCOTS PINE

Broadleaved woodlands

In a mature deciduous wood there are usually more trees of one species than of others. This is the species that grows best in a particular environment and is known as the **dominant species**. Woodlands are usually dominated by oak, beech, ash, alder or birch.

Oakwoods grow best on heavy, clay soils; beechwoods are usually on chalky slopes; ashwoods are found in limestone areas; alders grow best near water and in marshy areas; and birchwoods do well on poor sandy soil, often on high ground where few other species grow.

In some places there are **mixed woodlands**. Different kinds of trees such as oak, ash, beech and sycamore grow within a few metres of one another. Other trees such as rowan, holly, poplar and willow can also be found in woods, but they rarely become the dominant species.

The layers of a wood

Many kinds of plants other than trees grow in woods. They grow at different levels known as layers. Mosses and fungi grow on the lowest **ground layer;** flowers and ferns make up the **herb layers** above them. Higher up grow bushes, for example, hazel or elder. They form the **shrub layer.** Above this are the small trees like hawthorn or rowan. Their branches spread between the shrubs and taller dominant trees. This is the **under-storey.**

The leafy tops of the woodland trees form the highest layer known as the **canopy.**

See if you can spot these layers in a wood. They are clearest in oak, ash and birch woods. The canopy in beechwoods is usually thick, so little sunlight gets through and few plants of the lower layers can grow successfully.

Canopy

Under-storey

Shrub layer

Herb layer

Ground layer

Life in a broadleaved wood

This picture shows some of the animals and plants that can be found in broadleaved woods.

OAK

GREAT SPOTTED WOODPECKER

JAY

BEECH

GREY SQUIRREL

BLUEBELL

HOLLY

WOOD MOUSE

WOOD SORREL

WOOD ANEMONE

COMMON SHREW

CEP

A woodland diary

If you keep a record book of the changes you see in a wood during different seasons, you can make comparisons between one year and another. Use a ring binder for your diary so that you can add extra pages as you wish. Note down the date, weather conditions, and the plants and animals you find.

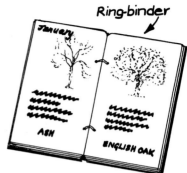

Ring-binder

Winter

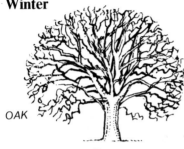

OAK

In winter, when deciduous trees have dropped all their leaves, their "skeleton" shape is easy to see.

You can also identify trees by looking at their winter buds.

OAK

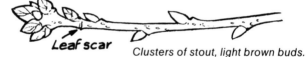

Leaf scar

Clusters of stout, light brown buds.

SYCAMORE

Leaf scar

Large, green buds with dark-edged scales; opposite pairs.

HAWTHORN

Sharp thorns. Smooth, grey stem.

You can collect specimens of winter buds, but also try to draw them and describe them in your diary. One of the field guides listed on page 59 will help you identify them.

Spring

Look for woodland flowers in the spring when broadleaved trees are still leafless and the flowers have enough sunlight to make them grow. Make charts like the ones below to record the flowering seasons of different plants. Then you can compare charts from different years and see the effect of different weather conditions.

1977	J	F	M	A	M	J	J	A	S	O	N	D
Primrose				▓	▓							
Bugle					▓	▓						
Wild Strawberry				▓	▓							

1978	J	F	M	A	M	J	J	A	S	O	N	D
Primrose			▓	▓								
Bugle					▓	▓						
Wild Strawberry			▓	▓								

On a separate page in your diary you can draw the flower. Make a note of where it is growing (under trees, on the edge of the wood, in a sunny glade, near water, etc.), whether the trees are in bud, flower or leaf and what the weather is like.

Also record when the trees in the wood begin to bud and flower.

Summer

Summer is the best time to study insects, birds and other animal life in woods. Look carefully on plant stems and the leaves of trees for caterpillars, spiders and grasshoppers.

Search the ground litter for beetles, millipedes, slugs and snails. Watch birds searching for insects or seeds for their young and see if you can spot the nests to which they take the food.

On or around fallen trees and rotting tree stumps are good places to look for wildlife. Gently lift pieces of loose bark to see what is sheltering beneath. Replace the bark carefully afterwards.

Bird's Nest Orchid

Grows in rotting matter on the woodland floor, often near fallen logs.

Nuthatch

Often seen on trees or logs, picking out insects and caterpillars.

Bracket fungus

This type of fungus gets its food from rotting wood. There are many different species that you can find.

Woodlouse
Shelters in damp places such as under loose bark or fallen logs. Feeds on rotting wood. 1 cm long.

Devil's Coach Horse
Feeds at night on small insects. Arches its tail over its head when disturbed. 2-3 cm long.

Autumn

In autumn, look for fruits and seeds. Compare their shapes and sizes and see whether they grow singly or in groups. This will help you identify different trees. Note when the fruits appear and when they are shed.

Autumn is also a good time to look for fungi on tree-trunks, decaying branches, fallen leaves and in grassy patches.

How seeds are scattered

The fruits and seeds of trees are carried away from the parent tree in many different ways. Some of them float and are carried by rivers and streams. Nuts and berries are taken as food by birds and animals. The seeds might then be dropped accidentally, passed out intact in droppings or thrown out after the surrounding fruit has been eaten. Below are some examples to look for.

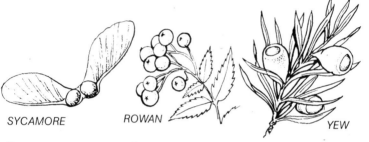

SYCAMORE   ROWAN   YEW

Sycamore fruits are in pairs with wings and spin away from the tree in the wind.

Birds eat **Rowan berries.** The seeds pass out in their droppings.

Birds eat the bright red **Yew berries** and drop the seeds.

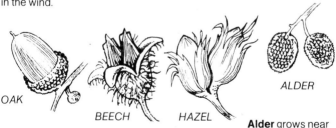

OAK   BEECH   HAZEL   ALDER

Oak acorns fall out of their cups and split to let the young root and shoot grow out.

Beechnuts and **hazelnuts** are dropped or buried by birds and animals.

Alder grows near water. The cone-like fruit stays on all winter. In spring the buoyant seeds fall out of the fruit and may float away.

Glossary

Bruising (of fungi) – when fungi are damaged through handling, the bruised parts may change colour. This is due to their juice being exposed to oxygen in the air.

Cocoon – the protective case which a pupa forms around itself.

Display flight – special flight, usually performed to attract a mate, but sometimes to threaten rival birds or to advertise ownership of territory.

Evergreen – tree or shrub which keeps its leaves in winter.

Frond – leaf of a fern (also the leaf-like part of a lichen or seaweed).

Fruit – the part of a plant that contains the seeds. It may be dry e.g. a nut, or fleshy e.g. a berry.

Gills (of fungi) – umbrella-like ribs or plates on the underside of a fungus cap. They bear many spores which fall to the ground or are carried away in the air.

Herb – plant with no hard, woody parts.

Invertebrates – animals without backbones e.g. slugs, insects.

Larva – the form which some animals take before they become adult, e.g. the caterpillar form of a butterfly.

Leaf-litter – rotting leaves and rotting plants which form a layer on the ground.

Mammals – warm-blooded animals which suckle their young.

Migrant – an animal which migrates.

Migration – movement of animals to another area, usually at a distance.

Milk (of fungi) – juice which drips from some fungi when they are touched. It may be clear, white or brightly coloured according to the species.

Nocturnal – active mostly at night.

Ovipositor – long, pointed organ at the hind end of female insects; used for laying eggs.

Pores (of fungi) – the round openings of tube-shaped gills on the underside of a fungus cap.

Pupa – the last form which an insect takes before it changes into an adult; it may have a hard, protective case.

Rump – the tail end (but not the tail) of an animal.

Runner (of a plant) – a stem which creeps along the ground. It grows roots at its tip and forms a new plant.

Sepal – small parts of a flower supporting the petals; usually green and leaf-shaped.

Sett – the burrow of a badger. It usually has many tunnels and entrances.

Shrub – plant with hard, woody stems (not a trunk), usually smaller than trees.

Species – nearly all the plants and animals in this book are individual species. All members of the same species, e.g. all Field Mice, can breed together and usually look alike.

Spore print – if the cap of a fungus is placed gill-side down on a piece of paper, the spores fall out of the gills and leave a pattern on the paper; this is usually coloured.

Spores – the reproductive parts of fungi, mosses and ferns. They take the place of seeds.

Wing cases (of insects) – moveable, hard parts of an insect's shell, covering the wings.

Books to read

Woodland Life. G. Mandahl-Barth (Blandford Press).

A Field Guide to the Trees of Britain and Northern Europe. A. Mitchell (Collins).

The NatureTrail Book of Trees & Leaves. I. Selberg (Usborne).

The RSPB Guide to British Birds. D. Saunders (Hamlyn).

A Field Guide to the Birds of Britain and Europe. R. T. Peterson, G. Mountford and P. A. D. Hollom (Collins).

The NatureTrail Book of Birdwatching Malcolm Hart (Usborne).

Mammals of Britain: Their Tracks, Trails and Signs. M. J. Lawrence and R. W. Brown (Blandford).

The Handbook of British Mammals. Edited by G. R. Corbet (Blackwell).

The NatureTrail Book of Wild Animals R. Harthill (Usborne).

Collins Guide to Mushrooms & Toadstools. Morten Lange & F. Bayard Hora (Collins).

The Wild Flowers of Britain and Northern Europe. R. Fitter, A. Fitter, M. Blamey (Collins).

The Concise British Flora in Colour. W. Keble Martin (Ebury Press/Michael Joseph).

The Oxford Book of Flowerless Plants. F. H. Brightman (Oxford).

British Butterflies: A Field Guide. R. Goodden (David & Charles).

The Observer's Book of Larger Moths. L. E. Ford (Warne).

The NatureTrail Book of Insect Watching. Thomson (Usborne).

A Field Guide to the Insects of Britain and Northern Europe. Chinery (Collins).

The Oxford Book of Invertebrates. D. Nichols, J. Cooke, D. Whiteley (Oxford).

The Ecology of Woodlands. A. Leutscher (Watts).

Clubs to join

The Royal Forestry Society of England, Wales and Northern Ireland. Anyone interested in trees and woodlands can join. Foresters and conservationists in the society work together to see that the growing of trees for timber does not upset the wildlife living in the woods. There are outdoor meetings in woodlands and lectures and visits for all members. In the *Quarterly Journal of Forestry* there are articles and book reviews on woodland subjects including wildlife. To find out more send a self-addressed, stamped envelope to 102 High Street, Tring, Herts.

British Naturalists' Association. It has regular field and indoor meetings for studying natural history. It has a magazine, *Country-side,* which has a special junior section. For membership details send a self-addressed, stamped envelope to Mrs Griffiths, 23 Oak Hill Close, Woodford Green, Essex, IG8 9PH.

The Watch Club (address: Watch, 22 The Green, Nettleham, Lincoln LN2 2NR) is sponsored by the Society for the Promotion of Nature Reserves and the *Sunday Times.* It has its own magazine, special projects and local groups for all areas. To find out more, send a self-addressed stamped envelope.

Get the address of your local **County Naturalist Trust** from the Council for Nature (The Zoological Society, Regent's Park, London NW1). Send a stamped, self-addressed envelope.

Scorecard

The plants and animals in this scorecard are arranged in alphabetical order.
When you spot a particular species, fill in the date next to its name. You can
add up your score after a day out spotting.

	Score	Date seen		Score	Date seen
Admiral, White	15		Bracken	5	
Agaric, Fly-	10		Bug, Common Shield	10	
Alder, Common	5		Bugle	10	
Anemone, Wood	10		Buzzard	15	
Ant, Wood	10		Capercaillie	20	
Aphid, Spruce	10		Cat, Wild	20	
Archangel, Yellow	10		Celandine, Lesser	5	
Ash, Common	5	MAY	Centipede	5	
Aspen	15		Cep	10	
Badger	15	DEC	Chaffinch	5	March
Beech, Common	5		Chanterelle	10	
Beetle, Ant-	15		Cherry, Wild	5	Feb
Beetle, Longhorn	15		Chestnut, Sweet	5	
Beetle, Elm Bark	10		Chiffchaff	10	
Beetle, Stag	15		Comma	15	
Beetle, Violet Ground	5		Cricket, Wood	15	
Birch, Silver	5		Crossbill	15	
Blackcap	15		Cuckoo Pint	10	
Blewit, Wood	10	DEC	Death-cap	15	
Bluebell	10	DEC	Deceiver	5	
Blue, Holly	10	Feb	Deer, Fallow	10	
Boletus, Bitter	15		Deer, Red	15	

	Score	Date seen		Score	Date seen
Deer, Roe	15		Marten, Pine	20	
Dormouse, Common	20		Mercury, Dog's	10	
Elder	5		Merveille-du-jour	15	
Emperor, Purple	25		Milk-cap, Red	10	
Fern, Hard	15		Milk-cap, Saffron	10	
Fern, Hartstongue	10		Millipede	10	
Firecrest	20		Moth, Bordered White	10	
Fir, European Silver	10		Moth, Goat	15	
Fly, Ichneumon	15		Moth, Leopard	15	
Flycatcher, Pied	15		Moth, Peppered	10	
Fox, Red	10		Moth, Pine Hawk	20	
Foxglove	15		Moth, Green Tortrix	5	
Fritillary, High Brown	5		Mouse, Wood	10	Jan 11/11
Fungus, Honey	5		Mouse, Yellow-necked Field	15	
Funnel-cap	15		Mushroom, Wood	15	
Glow-worm	15		Nettle	5	Apr
Goldcrest	10		Nightjar	15	
Hare, Brown	5		Nuthatch	15	
Hawthorn, Common	5		Oak, English	5	
Holly	5		Owl, Tawny	15	
Hornbeam	10		Paxil	5	
Hornet	10		Peach Blossom	10	
Jay	10		Periwinkle, Lesser	15	
Ladybird, Eyed	15		Pheasant	5	
Larch, European	5		Pine, Scots	5	

	Score	Date seen		Score	Date seen
Polecat	20		Stinkhorn	10	
Polypody	15		Strawberry, Wild	15	
Primrose	10	*Jan 18th*	Sycamore	5	
Rabbit	5		Tit, Coal	10	
Redpoll	15		Tit, Long-tailed	10	*DEC 30th*
Redstart	15		Tit, Marsh	15	
Robin	5	*DEC*	Treecreeper	10	
Rowan	5		Veil-cap, Tall	15	
Sawfly, Birch	10		Violet, Common Dog	10	
Scale Insect	10		Warbler, Garden	15	
Shrew, Common	10		Warbler, Willow	10	
Shrew, Pygmy	15		Warbler, Wood	15	
Sickener	10		Wasp, Giant Wood	15	
Siskin	15		Weevil, Leaf-rolling	10	
Snake-fly	15		Weevil, Nut	5	
Sorrel, Wood	5		Weevil, Pine	15	
Sparrowhawk	15		Willow, Goat	5	
Speckled Wood	5		Woodcock	15	
Spider, Crab	10		Woodpecker, Greater Spotted	10	
Spider, Garden	5		Woodpecker, Green	15	
Spider, Hunting	10		Woodpecker, Lesser Spotted	20	
Spider, Zebra	5		Woodpigeon	5	
Spruce, Norway	5		Woundwort, Wood	20	
Squirrel, Grey	5	*Jan first*	Yew	20	
Squirrel, Red	15	*Apr*			

Index